Friend Grief in the Workplace:

MORE THAN AN EMPTY CUBICLE

VICTORIA NOE

For a list of grief support resources: www.VictoriaNoe.com

Printed in the United States of America

First Printing, 2015

ISBNs
  978-0-9903081-3-3 (paperback)
  978-0-9903081-4-0 (epub)
  978-0-9903081-5-7 (mobi)

King Company Publishing – Chicago, IL 60618

Table of Contents

Dedication

To those with whom we share most of our waking hours, in the pursuit of a living, a calling and a better life.

Introduction:
Why Work Friends Matter

I am deeply sad to lose Gower as my director. I find it
unbearable to lose him as my friend.

> – Michael Stewart, writer, on hearing the news of Gower
> Champion's death

When I began writing the Friend Grief series, I worked off a
very simple premise: our friends are important to us, so we
grieve deeply when they die. I had no hard data to support that
premise. Everything in my books is anecdotal, stories told by the
surviving friends. But as I began work on this book, I felt that
I needed more. I wanted hard data to prove that the friends we
work with are important.

I searched online for weeks, checking human resources
organizations and grief support groups. I found a lot of policy
documents: how much paid bereavement leave is allowed for
someone who loses a friend (on the rare occasion that friends are
included in the bereavement policy, it's one day), how to generally

deal with an employee who is grieving, what your legal obligations are when an employee dies, how to keep business going when the boss dies. Very dry stuff, very unemotional, even when discussing the death of an employee. This was not what I was interested in using.

When I'd just about given up, I found an article in the *Chicago Tribune* about the results of a survey conducted in August 2014 by Globoforce, "the leading provider of social recognition solutions, helping companies build strong cultures of engaged employees through the power of thanks." In other words, they help large corporations design employee recognition programs.

Since 2011, they've surveyed full-time employees in the US twice a year regarding their work lives. They use that data to better serve their clients' needs.

They'd already acknowledged the impact of coworker relationships, but in the executive summary of their Fall, 2014 survey (*The Effect of Work Relationships on Organizational Culture and Commitment*), they admitted:

> Something we've noticed – but had not yet explored in depth – is the powerful relationships that underlie those work connections...

So, while most of their survey was focused on employee recognition programs, they began by asking 716 randomly selected full-time employees around the U.S. about the importance of their coworkers. Their summary concluded:

> Peer relationships are critical to the modern work experience. As we spend more time at work, we are investing more, emotionally and professionally, in

the relationships we make at work. They have become central to the quality of our lives.

What led them to make such a statement? Findings like these:

- 78% of employees who work 30-50 hours/week spend more time with colleagues than family.

- 95% have made at least one friend through work.

- 87% trust their coworkers.

- 73% have laughed so hard with co-workers that they almost cried.

- 61% have cried with coworkers.

- 89% say work relationships matter to their quality of life.

- Employees with work friends are twice as likely to trust company leadership.

Yet even with these findings, the death of a coworker/boss/employee is rarely discussed: not surprising, when you consider that death is a topic most people would rather avoid.

When you're at work, you're supposed to be working: no personal phone calls, no pining over a lost love, no two-hour lunches. Whatever is going on in your life outside of work is supposed to stay there. You are being paid to do your job, not conduct personal business.

But how do you function when your workplace is disrupted by the death of one of your coworkers, particularly one who has become a friend?

Some people have no choice because work is a matter of life or death: active duty military and first responders. They have to bury a normal grief for the people they work with because they're in a high stakes situation.

Most of us are luckier than that. We work in an office, a coffeehouse, a TV station, a school, a fitness center, a theatre. We work for a multi-national corporation or a mom-and-pop storefront. We work anonymously, out of sight of the public, or we are known to millions of people.

When one of your friends at work dies, you are plunged into a strange new reality. Not only is your personal life affected, but your work life is as well. Your work place has changed – maybe a little, maybe a lot. Maybe it wasn't a coworker who died: maybe it was your employee, or the boss, or the owner.

While you grieve the loss of your friend at work, you are faced with some pretty unsettling questions. You may feel selfish for even thinking them.

- Who's going to take up the slack?
- Where's their phone/laptop?
- How do I figure out what they were working on if I don't know their password?
- Who's going to clear out their stuff?
- Who's going to be promoted to their job?
- Who gets their office/parking space?
- Who's going to be my new boss?
- Will I still have a job?

What if your coworker died on the job? Would you still feel safe working there? The National Safety Council reported that slips, trips and falls are the leading cause of death in the workplace. Shootings in the workplace are sadly common, whether the result of a domestic dispute, or a disgruntled former employee. Terrorist attacks, such as 9/11, or natural disasters can also result in workplace deaths.

Whatever the situation, whatever the cause, none of these are bad questions. All of them are quite reasonable and will have to be addressed, some quickly. If the owner of your company died, it would be natural to wonder about your own job security.

What you might see, too, after the death of a coworker is some pretty disgusting behavior. People who didn't really know them will now be the loudest mourners. People will inflate the true nature of their relationship with the deceased.

Then there are those who will seek to profit by positioning themselves for a promotion. I've seen people do that after a coworker was fired or announced their resignation. But to behave that way after someone dies – and in many cases, a very short time after – can affect working relationships down the line.

Grief is hard and grief in the workplace affects us in ways we might not anticipate. It doesn't have to be a national tragedy like 9/11, or a traumatic event like a workplace shooting, to affect us.

You're going to meet some people now in a variety of professions. Some lost coworkers, some lost employees or employers. But all experienced a life-changing event: one that changed their perspective about their own future and the people around them – at work and beyond.

"Guess Who Died?"

When a tragic death impacts your workplace, the best place to turn would be your company crisis manual… If you don't have a crisis manual when a traumatic death occurs, pull together a team of key decision-makers immediately and craft a plan. Your plan should be compassionate and as thorough as possible.

– Alan D. Wolfelt, PhD, Healing Grief at Work

In moments of crisis we look to those in authority to take charge. The problem is that not every company has an employee handbook that includes what to do when one of their own dies. It may dictate dry policies, such as how to calculate accrued vacation time or when the last paycheck is cut. But rarely does it answer practical questions that require answers:

How should employees and customers be notified of the death?

Do employees have the right to paid time off to attend the funeral or memorial service?

> Should the company bring in grief counselors?
>
> When is it appropriate to clean out the person's desk and assign a replacement – and who should do it?

Not everyone wants to share health news with their friends. Some people don't even want to share it with family members. "I don't want you to worry" is the common refrain. Some don't want their friends to treat them differently. They don't want that kind of attention. Everyone has their own reasons to share or not to share.

When a friend at work is dying, their reasons for not telling others may be much more practical. They may fear not being able to keep up with their workload. They may fear being fired if they can't do their jobs as usual or need extra time off for doctor appointments. They may fear losing their insurance if they lose their job. They may simply need the money to pay their medical bills.

So you and others may be kept in the dark during this time. A lack of clear workplace policies – which could ease the mind of the friend who's dying – or simply a desire for privacy could keep everyone in the dark. It's not a surprise, then, that releasing the news that a friend at work is terminally ill or has died is often dictated by the friend themselves. Their decision can have a powerful impact on the workplace.

Monsignor Kenneth Velo was assigned to a Northwest-Side Chicago parish, Queen of All Saints, while working as a member of the archdiocese's priest placement board when Joseph Bernardin was appointed archbishop. Recognizing that Velo understood priests – and was trusted by them – Bernardin appointed him to the personnel board. In those first months, the new archbishop relied on Velo to help him get to know his priests.

In fact, that dependence grew, and Velo was asked to leave his parish while remaining on the personnel board. Now he would take on the duties of executive assistant to the new cardinal, what Velo referred to as "a ministry to one."

Velo moved into the stately mansion on the edge of Lincoln Park, home to the head of the Chicago archdiocese. It is used for meetings and small events, but upstairs it was home to the cardinal, his assistant and a few other staff members.

For a time, Velo made sure their relationship was strictly business, maintaining a separate group of friends. He told me he consciously resisted becoming friends with his boss. As much as he loved his job, he did not want to become too attached: priests serve wherever they are told. He knew he could be reassigned at any time, anywhere that the cardinal determined. But as time passed, working together closely, enjoying each other's company, they became friends. There was a strong bond between them, a trust that was rooted in Velo's knowledge that the cardinal was the same person in his rooms on the third floor as he was in a press conference.

Joseph Cardinal Bernardin, archbishop of Chicago, opted to be transparent about his 1995 pancreatic cancer diagnosis, treatment and subsequent recurrence. He believed these were teachable moments for his flock and for his city, so he lived what he always tried to preach. In doing so, he delivered a powerful lesson in grace.

He never downplayed the seriousness of his illness. In fact, he allowed his doctors to speak to the press. Such transparency is rare, even in public figures. But Bernardin saw his illness as part of his ministry. If he was indeed a teacher, a leader, he had to set the example. His treatments, his hospital stays, his death: all were shared with the world.

Perhaps because of his openness, Catholics and non-Catholics alike felt a bond with the cardinal. Strangers meeting him for the first time felt close enough to call him "Joe"- though Velo never called him anything but "Eminence" or "Cardinal." The local media – along with the public -conducted a vigil outside his residence when word came that Bernardin was close to death. When his body lay in state for two days at Holy Name Cathedral, almost 200,000 Chicagoans lined up to pay their respects. His funeral was broadcast live on TV and radio. And Monsignor Velo gave a homily that is remembered to this day, in large part because of his theme, which reinforced Bernardin's openness: "Didn't he teach us? Didn't he show us the way?"

The cathedral was full of cardinals and archbishops, politicians and family members who came to Chicago from around the world. In fact, Velo poked fun at being chosen, introducing himself with the nickname given him by Cardinal Bernardin's mother: "I'm the 'regular' driver."

Why was Velo given that particular honor? On their last flight home back to Chicago from Rome just two months before he died, Bernardin wrote four pages of instructions for his death and funeral, which included the following notation:

> Homilist: Monsignor Kenneth Velo. I am confident that he will express adequately my life and ministry.

Velo objected; the honor and responsibility felt overwhelming, but he was overruled by his boss. He told me that in the end that assignment freed him to say what was in his heart.

Other people in the public eye are not necessarily as open about their health as Bernardin was. Perhaps it's only fitting that two of the most dramatic stories of telling employees of the death of their boss come from Broadway.

Bob Fosse – the director and/or choreographer of such Broadway classics as *Chicago*, *Pippin* and *Pajama Game*, as well as Academy Award winning director of *Cabaret* – died on opening night of the Washington, DC, pre-Broadway opening of his revival of *Sweet Charity*. His ill health had been an open secret for years. He rarely spoke of it (other than to make an allegorical film, *All That Jazz*, about his life and death), but those closest to him knew. His professional attitude and excellence inspired a fierce, protective loyalty from his fans, dancers, ex-wives, current and previous girlfriends.

A perfectionist to the end, he worked everyone hard in the show's final rehearsal that day. He called a break around 5:00, asking everyone to take a seat in the house. They expected his traditional "just do the show, no more, no less" opening night speech. Instead, they got a final lesson from him, an uncharacteristically long twenty minute sharing of wisdom and hope. In Sam Wasson's definitive biography, *Fosse*, Lisa Embs, a dancer in the show, recalled:

> As Bob was talking to us that day, I remember thinking it was like he was reciting his last will and testament. He was talking about how difficult our lives are in terms of the life of an artist, in terms of trying to take care of daily things like rent and family, and where's our next job, our self-esteem, and that even though it didn't always feel like it, what we're doing is worth something.
>
> He said, "I would do anything to make this show a success."

Two hours later, he was dead of a massive heart attack.

In keeping with perhaps the most famous showbiz tradition – "the show must go on" – the cast was notified after the performance, just before leaving for what would now be a somber cast party. It was not just the death of their director – it was the end of an era in musical theatre.

His death was, though, somewhat anticlimactic – and Fosse would undoubtedly agree. Though he was mourned by theatre professionals and fans all over the world, his death did not rise to the surreal drama that surrounded the earlier death of his friend and competitor, Gower Champion.

Champion had been in a self-imposed exile in California when the opportunity to return to Broadway presented itself in the form of *42nd Street*. An homage to the classic understudy-makes-her-Broadway-debut-when-the-leading-lady-gets-hurt-opening-night storyline, the show was a stage version of the 1933 film starring Ruby Keeler. Champion, who was already ill, found new strength and purpose in the project, passion that would infect everyone around him, including those who had worked with him before, like Jerry Orbach:

> I could talk to him. I could give him an idea, discuss it, and invent things, like pulling out Peggy's lucky scarf at the end; whereas in 1961 (during *Carnival!*), everyone was deathly afraid of him. But now he was much more approachable and would exchange ideas. Of course, none of us knew how sick he was. I still don't know to this day if *he* knew how sick he was! I think it was one of the great acting jobs ever.

With a maniacal attention to detail (at least on the musical numbers – he had little time or patience for the spoken scenes), Champion made an impression on all who worked on the show. During the Washington tryout, he waited to speak to Jon Engstrom, one of the cast members. For all his bravado, Champion was – like his contemporary Bob Fosse – often painfully shy. He complimented the man on his performance in a particular number, "Shadow Waltz," insisting that it always generated applause. Engstrom objected, but his director insisted.

> "Well, every time I've seen it, it's gotten applause," replied Gower with a smile. "I just want to tell you that I really appreciate the work you put into that, and thank you." Then he disappeared. Ill as he was, Gower had come all the way down into the dressing room area to speak with him – all the more reason why the compliment made a lasting impression on the dancer.

With the show in previews in New York, Champion's health faded quickly. He was hospitalized and died the morning of *42nd Street's* opening. Producer David Merrick swore family, friends and hospital staff to secrecy until after the performance that night.

The opening was a huge success – twelve curtain calls. At the end of the last one, Merrick walked out on stage from the wings.

> Shaking his head, he raised his hand for quiet: "I'm sorry to have to report…"

> Again the house went mad. Sorry? Sorry for what? He was baiting then by acting like he had a flop. A typical Merrick ploy. They lapped it up.

> "No, no, it's very tragic," he insisted, raising his voice against the persistent laughter.

> "You don't understand. Gower Champion died this morning."

The audience and cast gasped. Jerry Orbach yelled to the stage manager to bring down the curtain. Silence filled the theatre. Amid the chaos backstage, there was the realization that the opening night party was now a wake.

As you can imagine, not everyone approved of the dramatic way Merrick notified the world, including the cast. Many felt they should've been told before the performance. Others believed Champion would've enjoyed the extreme theatricality of the announcement.

Bob Fosse, who hated being upstaged, admitted to Lee Roy Reams, one of the show's stars:

> Gower once again did me one better. I filmed my death. Gower Champion had the nerve to do it on opening night.

And even though Fosse, too, died on the opening night of his show, the circumstances did not compare for sheer theatricality.

Public and private grief intersect on television as well as theatre. If you visit the office of the local CBS affiliate in Chicago, you'll see two pictures on Roseanne Tellez's desk, both of her with her former on-air partner Randy Salerno. They're both laughing in the pictures. That's because in addition to working together for 16 years at WBBM and WGN, they shared a deep friendship, too.

Tellez has the distinction of being the first person I ever interviewed at length for my books. She was gracious and open about the loss of Salerno – and apologetic whenever she got emotional talking about him.

"He was a good friend – like a girlfriend." Their families were close: he danced with her mother at Tellez's wedding reception. Rather than showcase his professional awards, his office walls were filled with family photos and his kids' art projects. Salerno and Tellez shared an on-air chemistry that earned them loyal viewers, who enjoyed their professionalism as well as the times he would try to make her laugh. "He was a goofball," she remembered, but a consummate professional as well. "I got to laugh through my workday."

Salerno was not due to come to work that morning in January 2008, so Tellez was on-air without him. But during a commercial break, her producer called her off the set to give her the stunning news: Salerno had been killed the night before in a snowmobiling accident in Wisconsin. The show went on, but not with her.

The loss of her friend and partner was difficult to process. She insists it didn't really hit her until Salerno's wife came into the office a few weeks later to clean out his desk.

Tellez didn't return to the set that morning, so the news of his death was announced by others on camera. Even as Salerno's coworkers struggled to accept his death, they still had to prepare the broadcasts. For the rest of the day and for several days after, morning and evening news shows – including those on other networks included tributes to the respected and well-liked Salerno.

Is there a good time to break the news of a coworker's death? As we've seen above with Cardinal Bernardin, sometimes the coworker controls the flow of information. In the case of a sudden death, the person in charge of the workplace might make the announcement. In the cases of Fosse, Champion and Salerno, the decision was made to carry on work as usual. But that's not always easy because sometimes that death takes place right before your eyes.

Dan Wheldon, the British-born two-time Indianapolis 500 winner, died in a horrific crash at Las Vegas Motor Speedway in October, 2011. The 33-year old left behind a wife and two small children.

In the months following Wheldon's death, grief counseling was provided for the drivers through Bob Hills, a chaplain with IndyCar Ministries. You might think that such a stereotypically macho culture would resist counseling. But like any serious athletes, they embraced it: not just for the personal need, but for the professional need. Because in a few months, they'd have to race again. Many also leaned on each other for support. Some texted or called their friends more often. A few even reached out to settle feuds.

Five months later, many of those same drivers gathered for the opening of the 2012 IndyCar season – in St. Petersburg, where Wheldon had lived. For some, it was their first time there since Wheldon's funeral.

Not surprisingly, the weekend was filled with memorials: pregame ceremony, orange ribbons (a tribute to his car) sold to raise money for the Alzheimer's Foundation, even Turn 10 was christened "Dan Wheldon Way."

Part of the television coverage included frequent replays of the fiery crash that took his life, to recap the tragedy for viewers.

His fellow drivers needed no reminders: they witnessed the crash.

Few sports are as dangerous or competitive for individuals as car racing. Though occasionally someone in the stands is hurt, it's the drivers who are constantly at risk. They know this. You might think that racecar drivers – like others who participate in dangerous professions – have a death wish. Certainly the adrenaline feeds them. They like the excitement. But death wish? No.

Perhaps it's that shared risk – as well as the thrill – that creates a bond between them. So the drivers who gathered to open the season didn't have to watch the replays of Wheldon's last moments to remember.

His friends – his coworkers – now had to focus on doing the thing they loved. The thing Dan Wheldon loved.

The thing that killed him.

The thing they know could kill them, too.

When the time came to go back to work – to endure the memorials at St. Petersburg and again two months later at the Indy 500 – they couldn't forget about Wheldon even if they wanted to. But for the moment, there was a race to run.

They Come in Threes –
Don't They?

Death comes in threes, or so they say. Often when two celebrities die within a short amount of time, many of us have wondered out loud "Who will be the third?"

The New York Times conducted an analysis in August, 2014, in an attempt to debunk this urban myth. Using a two thousand-word obituary as its baseline (fallible, but as good a measurement as any of "celebrity" – 449 people met the criteria), it found that between 1990 and 2014, in only seven cases did three celebrities die within five days of each other. That would be considered statistically random, not significant. Another urban myth shattered, though it probably won't stop anyone from waiting for that third death.

A short time after this survey was reported, the Chicago theatre community would have given anything to have suffered the loss of only three of its members in the week beginning Labor Day weekend. Between August 31 and September 6, 2014, the community was rocked by the deaths of props designer Joel

Lambie, actors Sati Ward and Trinity P. Murdock, along with WGN personality and theatre lover Roy Leonard. But it was the shocking deaths of respected actors Molly Glynn and Bernie Yvon in separate accidents on the morning of September 6 that brought everyone to their knees. "It feels like God is against us today," mourned one community member.

The Chicago theatre community is unique. I joined it in 1977, after graduate school, a time when David Mamet, John Malkovich, Gary Sinise, Bill Peterson and others defined the Chicago off-loop theatre movement. The style was gritty, emotional, in your face. It reflected the character of the city (for better or worse) and was unlike what was happening in the rest of the country. Soon people were coming to Chicago to find out what was going on, and trying to add "Chicago" to their resumes.

It's a close-knit community, more supportive than in places like New York, though just as competitive. Our trade association, the League of Chicago Theatres (of which I was a founding board member) includes not just Equity theatres, but non-Equity, community and educational theatres. Commit to your craft, don't be a diva, and you're welcome here.

That sense of community was never more evident than in the aftermath of these shocking losses. Rehearsals, like the one Yvon was driving to when he was killed, were cancelled. Funds were set up for the surviving families. Those who had worked with the ones who died spoke of their colleagues' dedication to excellence in their jobs and mentoring those new to the profession. For the first time in anyone's memory, the lights were dimmed not just at theatres in Chicago and the suburbs, but Milwaukee Repertory Theatre, where Glynn was scheduled to make her debut later in the season.

But theatre people, as a profession, are expected to channel their grief: "the show must go on," right? They're not the only ones.

June 22, 2002 was a good day to be a St. Louis Cardinals fan. After a bumpy start, we'd been in first place since pitcher Darryl Kile won the game on Tuesday. I was at home that Saturday morning, finishing some cleaning before settling down to watch my team face the Cubs at Wrigley Field. Now and then I'd turn on the TV for the pre-game show. At first, it didn't register: the game wasn't starting on time. That was more than unusual, but the reason the game was eventually cancelled would shock the baseball world: the thirty-three-year-old pitcher had died in his sleep from a heart attack.

It was a double tragedy for Cardinals Nation: their long-time, beloved broadcaster Jack Buck had died earlier that week. Buck was a link to the old days, a former on-air partner with Harry Caray, the man who'd made an emotional speech at the first game played after 9/11. He was a man who mentored many, a man of infinite grace and professionalism. And though he'd been ill for some time, his death was deeply mourned by those who worked with him in and out of the broadcast booth. The team attended a public memorial at Busch Stadium before leaving for the weekend series in Chicago.

Kile's death, however, was a body blow to his teammates and coaches. They were not even at the halfway point of the season. Though that game was cancelled, they had to keep the rest of the 162 game schedule beginning with Sunday. Kile's jersey, number 57, hung in the dugout at the end of the bench, and the ESPN cameras focused on it often. How would they get through the game under these circumstances?

Whether to play that Sunday game was a topic of passionate debate in the clubhouse. Catcher Mike Matheny was among those who advocated for cancelling the games and returning immediately to St. Louis. He was Kile's catcher. In fact, Kile refused to pitch unless Matheny was catching, and Kile was scheduled to pitch on that Sunday. Matheny told manager Tony LaRussa, "If Darryl's not pitching, I'm not catching."

This situation a good example of how people respond to death, especially sudden death. Some, like LaRussa, whose opinion prevailed, believe the world should go on, no matter how deep the grief. Others, like Matheny, can't imagine how that's possible. But both were able to get what they wanted: the nationally televised game was played with the battery made up of pitcher Jason Simontacchi and backup catcher Mike DiFelice, a game the Cardinals lost 8–3.

Professional athletes are a superstitious lot: refusing to shave during playoff runs, elaborate pre-game rituals, etc. Every season, on the Cardinals' annual trip to New York, Matheny used to buy a $15 knockoff watch from a sidewalk vendor. He tried to make it last until returning to the city the following season. In 2000, the day Kile won his twentieth game of the season, Matheny found a real Rolex on his chair in the locker room, a gift from Kile.

Sitting in front of his locker a few hours after being told of Kile's death, Matheny pulled the stem from the watch, stopping the time. He still owns the watch but hasn't worn it or replaced the stem.

He said he never will.

Those of us who are St. Louis Cardinals fans worried "That's two – who's next?" Luckily, it was one of those times when the superstition did not come true. Other Cardinal players have died since then – Josh Hancock in 2007, Oscar Taveras in 2014 – but not in threes or even twos. Not every workplace is as lucky.

On September 11, 2001, 343 firefighters rushed to the World

Trade Center and didn't return. Twelve ladder companies and three engine companies lost every person who answered the call that day. Of the five rescue companies that responded to the attack on the North Tower, no one survived. Not just rank and file were lost: 46 lieutenants, 21 captains, 23 chiefs, including the chief of department and a chaplain, Father Mychal Judge.

Everyone who reported for duty at the popular restaurant Windows on the World died that day, seventy-three in all. Many people who were not scheduled to work that day watched their televisions in horror as the towers fells: killing their coworkers and destroying their workplace. But percentage-wise, few companies located in the twin towers suffered losses comparable to Cantor Fitzgerald, which lost 658 of the 960 employees who worked there.

In addition to the emotional toll, all of these situations where people lost more than one coworker are reflected in the staggering loss of institutional memory. Think of your own workplace. There are people who know where things are, how things are done (in a way that's not written down in any employee manual), what's been tried before. "Go ask so-and-so. She knows where it is." But now they're gone – your boss, your employee, your coworker: your friend. And to make it worse, it's not only the loss of one friend. It's two or three or a dozen or a hundred or more.

For the New York City Fire Department, there was one small comfort. One of the things that had been known but never formally written down was the department's procedure after the death of a firefighter. Everybody knew what to do, but nothing was written down until the summer of 2001. Yes, you read that right. After 9/11, facing the prospect of funerals for 343 of its members, the comfort of those rituals – now known to all and available – helped those for whom the grief was immeasurable.

When dozens or hundreds of coworkers die, you have no time to process this because you still have a job to do – at least in the short-term. But you can't help but wonder about your own future. You hate feeling that selfish, that callous, but why wouldn't you worry? For those who worked in the twin towers, they didn't even have an office or store or coffee shop to go back to. Sometimes those businesses were relocated, as was the case with Cantor Fitzgerald. But some businesses did not survive. It's hard enough to lose the friends you worked with. The people who worked there not only lost their friends, not only lost their workplace, but lost their jobs, too.

"We Used to Work Together"

From 1989 to 1990 I worked at Chicago House, raising money for their residential programs for people living with HIV/AIDS. There were six of us in the office: four men, two women. None of them died while I worked there, but within a few years, three of the men were dead.

Death was all around us: clients, coworkers, friends in the community. At work I made friends somewhat unwillingly – not because the people I worked with weren't nice (though some weren't), but because I knew some of them would not live long and I didn't want to get attached.

Steve was my assistant. He was younger, taller, adorable and a much nicer human being than I'll ever be. He was also HIV+, and in 1989, that meant something very different than today. I needed an assistant who could do the heavy lifting – sometimes literally. I needed one who could put in twelve and fourteen hour days when we had big events. I actually advocated against his hiring because I was very aware of the physical stress the job would put on him. But I was outvoted.

I enjoyed working with Steve. It was impossible not to like him. But I kept my distance, emotionally. It was a few months after I left the job that his health began to deteriorate. I visited him once, to give his partner a few hours respite. We sat in the living room. I remember he was on the couch, bundled up to keep warm, and I sat across from him. Steve had dementia, and during that visit he sometimes talked gibberish, keeping eye contact with me the entire time. I had no idea what he was saying, but I made sure he had my attention.

At one point, he became lucid and asked, "So, do you think I'm crazy?" What I really wanted to do was cry, but instead I deflected his serious question with a joke: "No more so than usual." He laughed too. That was the last time I saw him alive. But the time apart did little to lessen my grief when he died in 1992.

I know what you're thinking: How could I grieve for someone I hadn't seen in months or even years? Because, like it or not, we remember.

We remember the late nights and weekends we worked with our friends, exhausted and cranky but loyal to a cause.

We remember the client lunches and Christmas parties and sharing a cab when it was too late to take the subway home alone.

We remember the hundreds of hours we spent sitting in adjacent cubicles, tossing papers over the divider at each other, and debating who would make the next Starbucks run.

As it turns out, being physically or even emotionally separated for a period of time doesn't guarantee that you won't grieve.

Trudy Ring, a volunteer at Chicago House, had a strategy. She decided not to volunteer at any of our residences. She was afraid of getting close to those who lived there, and wasn't willing to face the potential loss of any friends. As it turned out, her strategy only worked to a point. She spent her time in our office and became friends with Ernest, the volunteer director. She still grieves over his death in 2004.

As was the case with Trudy and Ernest, maybe your friendship lasted longer than the work relationship. Maybe your friendship faded once your work relationship ended. It might be reasonable, then, to assume that your grief would be muted. In fact, it might not.

Lynne McCollum Staley began working in the development and communications department at United Charities (now Metropolitan Family Services) in Chicago in 1985. A year later, Trici Brennan Zuba joined the team. They became fast friends, the kind of friends who spend hours talking about making the world a better place – through their jobs and their personal lives.

Eventually Staley transferred to the organization's suburban office to be closer to home and her two young sons. Zuba left to start her own public relations business. Still, their friendship remained strong. After Zuba's eighteen-month old daughter died from hemolytic uremic syndrome in 1990, Staley and her husband were the first to invite the Zuba's over for dinner.

On New Year's Day 1999, Trici Brennan Zuba died of a heart attack. Staley learned the news when she checked her voice mail upon return from vacation.

> The news literally sent me to my knees. I had been out
> of town and I found her obituary, with her gorgeous
> face, in that morning's Chicago *Tribune*.

The depth of her grief took her by surprise, and even Zuba's husband, Tom, seemed puzzled. "What are your tears about?" he asked her.

Eventually, she recognized what her friend's death had done to her:

> There was something new about me, in the days following her burial. There was a new awareness and understanding of what matters. Everything was brighter. I "got" things I had resisted. I started to saying "no" to things and "yes" to others.

What she didn't know yet was that grieving her friend, her former coworker, would push her into an entirely new direction, as you'll see later.

In his book *Waging Heavy Peace*, rock legend Neil Young insists that his best records were those produced by David Briggs. He hadn't seen Briggs for a while when he visited him in San Francisco in 1995. All he knew was that his friend had been sick, with his second bout of "something". There were no facts, just rumors, because Briggs wasn't one to share personal information easily. But once Young arrived, it was obvious that Briggs was dying.

Young asked him for advice about his music, going forward. Briggs replied with his signature phrase: "Be great or be gone." Young has kept that advice with him to this day.

> He was the most influential person on my music of anyone I've met. His guidance and friendship through the creation of countless pieces of music are one of the greatest gifts of my life, right up there with my wife's love and all of my children. I feel the loss. I feel the memories. I feel the weight of every mistake I made in our long relationship, the times he was right and I was wrong, the times I didn't use him to produce for the

wrong reason, every battle we had. I feel the absence of his unbelievable energy for music, combined with mine. There is no replacement for that. It is one of life's little voids.

Sometimes you don't realize the magnitude of a coworker's influence until after they're gone. Maybe you thanked them for helping us with a project or writing a recommendation. But did you ever tell them how much of a difference they made?

We all get annoyed during awards season when the winners rattle off dozens of names of people who helped them achieve that particular honor. But if you listen closely, you'll often hear them close with a tribute to someone who is no longer alive. Sometimes it's a parent. But often it's someone they worked with, a person who made an impression on them in the early days of their career: the person who gave them their first break because they believed in them.

Why thank them at an awards ceremony? Two reasons, I think. First, it's a fitting way to honor someone who helped you achieve the level of excellence for which you are now being recognized. And second, you feel the guilt of realizing you never thanked them while they were alive.

Thinking in terms of what was lost – not just the person, but their work – also comes up in Young's story about musician and songwriter Danny Whitten. Young wanted him in his band, for his first tour after his *Harvest* album was released. He'd heard Whitten – whose addiction to heroin is related in Young's "The Needle and the Damage Done" – was clean and doing well. But it became clear as soon as rehearsals began that Whitten had replaced heroin with alcohol, and was in no shape to tour. Young let him go with a plane ticket and a ride to the airport. The music had to come first, so he felt he had no choice.

That very night, the Los Angeles County coroner's office called Young: Danny had overdosed on alcohol and Valium.

> I knew that what I had done may have been a catalyst for Danny's death, but I also knew that there was really nothing else I could have done. I can never really lose that feeling. I wasn't guilty, but I was responsible in a way. It's part of what I do. Managing the band and taking care of the music is very painful at times. It's a sad story. A moment I will never forget, years I can never replace, music the world will never hear, all gone in the turning of a second.

That's a lot of guilt.

In the 1980's film *The Big Chill*, the friends gathered for Alex' funeral wonder what happened to him in the time since they'd lost contact with him. What drove him to suicide? One even assumes he could somehow have kept Alex alive, an assertion the others quickly shoot down.

People drift in and out of our lives all the time: we leave school, change jobs, move across the country. Like the characters in that film, the people in this chapter who'd lost touch may grieve, but feel no guilt about the separation.

Would any of them do things differently if they'd known how little time remained? Maybe. Maybe not. Often nothing could've changed the outcome,

But they still grieve and feel a deep sense of loss: for the laughter, the camaraderie and the music that's lost forever.

Even Nuns Have Friends
at Work

When I first had the idea for this book, I knew that I would use a very broad definition of work place. Actually "more than an empty cubicle" popped into my mind early on. That became my focus.

The barista who creates your latte, the teacher at school, the yoga instructor at the gym: they all work in places that are not offices. There's no desk in a high-rise dozens of stories tall. If we ever have occasion to think about people who work in the businesses we patronize, we probably have never given any thought to the friendships they make at work.

Two coffeehouses in Chicago suffered the same great loss, that of a beloved coworker. In each case, a young barista was killed in accident involving her bicycle and a car or truck. Both women were well known to customers and friends, loved by those they worked with and for. To most people a barista is someone you see every morning, but otherwise don't think much about. Their loss was a blow to their coworkers and customers; years later, memorials are still set up in each coffeehouse.

And that's just it: we have work friends who we see every day, work friends we talk to on the phone or email, work friends we see only occasionally, and work friends we've never met in person. Most of us do make friends in the workplace. But there was one workplace that I didn't think about until I wrote this book.

When I was growing up, it never crossed my mind that nuns had friends. Oh, sure, they lived together in a convent, worked together, traveled together, but somehow the human aspect was lost on me. Maybe it was because when I was young they still wore habits, which always set them apart and above the rest of us. But by high school, I not only saw evidence of those friendships, but I also learned of one that was especially unique.

Sister Mary Luke Tobin was the head of the Sisters of Loretto, the order of nuns who taught me for thirteen years. She loomed large, in part by virtue of being the first woman to serve as an official auditor at Vatican II in 1964. Often our teachers would tell a story that went "Mary Luke did this. Mary Luke did that." And whatever she did always seemed larger than life and all the more impressive considering the restrictions on women in general and nuns in particular at that time.

The friendship I learned about was the one she shared with Thomas Merton, the Trappist monk who resided at the Abbey of Our Lady of Gethsemani, twelve miles down a scenic, very winding road from the Loretto Motherhouse in Nerinx, Kentucky. They met at Loretto in October, 1960.

Merton was the author of sixty books, including what is arguably his most famous, *The Seven Storey Mountain*, the tale of his youth, conversion to Catholicism and entry into the Trappist order at Gethsemani. The contemplative life is one largely removed from the outside world, but not from personal contact.

He craved friendships, even in the monastery: not superficial ones, but those infused with intellectual curiosity and integrity.

The 1984 book *Merton: By Those Who Knew Him Best*, grew from the PBS documentary, *Merton*. In both, an impressive variety of friends such as Lawrence Ferlinghetti, Joan Baez, the Dalai Llama and Thich Nhat Hanh recount the impact of their friendships with Merton. One of the contributors was Sister Mary Luke.

They were very similar personalities: intellectual yet passionate, affable yet devoted to their vocations. Both were interested in the issues of the day, notably racism, peace and justice. Merton was ahead of his time – and his church – in many ways, warning of the spread of nuclear weapons, racism and war. It was on these issues, as well as deep discussions of spirituality and vocation, that their working friendship was based. United by these common causes, he saw Sister Mary Luke as:

> ...not only an intellectual equal and a woman spiritually in sympathy with [my] vocation, but a fellow worker for peace and justice.

In the documentary, she described their working friendship:

> I appreciate having had the pleasure of knowing him, the delight of having him come into a room, smiling, welcoming, filled with interest about everything in the world, looking for my response. Who could help but love this man? He was never a "guru" to me, but rather a good friend with whom I could exchange ideas, and I value that greatly.

And that, to me, is the definition of the perfect coworker.

"Back to Work, People!"

Accept that someone new will eventually fill that empty space. Although it may be unthinkable to imagine that someone irreplaceable will be replaced, it must eventually happen. Employees need to accept that someone new will fill that position and, possibly, sit in the chair of their departed colleague. The new person has some big shoes to fill, so they should feel welcomed and supported.

> – John McFerran, PhD, F.CHRP, Managing Director
> of Boyden Global Executive Search

The pilot of *LA Law* didn't do much to endear people to lawyers. The show opens early the morning after Labor Day. One of the secretaries, Roxanne, discovers the source of the bad smell in the office: the body of one of the firm's partners. She led her boss, Arnie Becker to the dead man's office, where she assures him:

> "I didn't actually touch him, but I'm pretty sure he's dead."

"If he is, I've got dibs on this office."

Then there's the partners' meeting later that morning, where the managing partner frets:

> "His passing leaves a serious void in an extremely lucrative part of our business."

In showing the in-fighting for the dead man's corner office, *LA Law* certainly perpetuated the stereotype of cold-hearted lawyers.

As you can imagine, after Cardinal Bernardin's funeral, Monsignor Velo's life changed dramatically. For a short time, he wasn't the man behind the cardinal anymore: he was in the public eye. He filled his time with work and speaking engagements.

He still lived in the mansion, but now with a new boss, Francis Cardinal George, a man who could not have been more different than Bernardin. Velo was asked to stay on the personnel board, to help George in the same way he'd helped Bernardin. But eventually he moved out and devoted all of his time to the Catholic Extension Society, where he'd been assigned eighteen months before Bernardin's death.

Time moved on. Velo is often asked to give speeches and sometimes opens with a disclaimer:

> Your pastor wants me to talk about Cardinal Bernardin,
> but it's been seventeen years and people say "get a life".
> But at the same time, he had such a profound impact,
> they want me to tell the stories.

So even though it's been almost twenty years now since his boss died, Monsignor Velo knows they will always be connected.

No one will think of him without recognizing his working friendship with Bernardin.

When a friend dies, you probably didn't hear a lot of people say "You need to find a new friend right away to replace them." That would be insensitive and inaccurate, assuming that any friend can be replaced. But when you work with a friend who died, eventually their job will be filled by someone else. And that can be a very sensitive situation.

These situations don't get any more public than the death of the late Tim Russert, NBC News Washington bureau chief and host of *Meet the Press*. Boston born and bred, he was nevertheless identified with his adopted home, Washington, DC. He began his career as an aide to Senator Daniel Patrick Moynihan, then to New York Governor Mario Cuomo. But it was when he made the switch to television that he became a fixture on the Washington political scene.

His sudden death in 2008, after a family trip to Italy celebrating his son's college graduation, set the best and worst of Washington society in motion. In addition to the private Catholic funeral, an invitation-only memorial service was held at a venue no less impressive than The Kennedy Center. It was attended by former (Bill Clinton), future (Barack Obama) and aspiring (too long a list) presidents and was broadcast live on MSNBC.

Even during the broadcast, as colleagues described the event, there was speculation about the motives of those attending. On their list was the desire of some people to be considered as the next host of *Meet the Press*. And though it may strike you as disrespectful to Russert's memory, he'd been in Washington long enough that he would not have been surprised. He may have even been entertained.

That is not to say that there weren't coworkers there who were genuinely distraught at his passing: there were. In speaking to a couple of his MSNBC colleagues five years later, I saw them still so deeply affected by the loss that the mention of Russert's name evokes a sudden and genuine sadness.

On MSNBC's broadcast, *Remembering Tim Russert,* his coworkers gathered after his death to reminisce about the man they worked with, the man they all considered a friend. Friendship and loyalty to those friends is a rarity in Washington, DC, as Mary Matalin pointed out:

> He never left anybody. He stood up for his friends, and it wasn't that we just loved him. He loved his friends and took care of them. And unlike most of this town, which is transactional, you weren't just his friend when you were in. If you were out of office, he still called you and he still – he just was loved because he was such a lover of people.

Even so, despite the type of person Russert was, there was still a fierce bidding war going on at the memorial service and in the days to come. Russert was gone, but his job was available.

No such obvious bidding war took place when Chicago local CBS news anchor Randy Salerno was killed in a snowmobile accident. But he and Roseanne Tellez were a team and the team was broken up. How do you carry on when your work identity is changed because your friend died? In that case, duties were reassigned and eventually new staff members were hired who didn't know Salerno. That can be a surprising but devastating trigger: when you realize that you now work with people who didn't know, much less care about, your friend. Like it or not, that is your new reality.

But the quote at the beginning of this chapter should give you pause. Imagine if you were that person. Maybe you were promoted or reassigned from within the company. Maybe you're a new hire. At some point in the interview process you became aware that you were replacing someone who died.

Imagine walking in your first day in the new job. If it were a normal situation, you would be a little nervous, but expect to be welcomed. You wouldn't expect your new coworkers to look at you with resentment at best, and possibly even hostility.

It's not your fault. You didn't kill their friend and coworker. But your presence confirms as nothing else can that that person is never coming back.

The boss is probably breathing a sigh of relief, secure in the knowledge that now things can finally get back to normal. Everyone can go back to work. We can all move on. If only it were that easy.

Tributes to Coworkers

Professional athletes who play on teams are assigned a number for their uniform. Sometimes, if a player was one of those rare talents, their number is retired: no other player can ever wear that number. When Michael Jordan was at his peak, wearing number 23 was seen as both a tribute to him, and a declaration of comparable talent. On a very few occasions, there's a much more personal attachment to a number.

When Jason Heyward made the opening day roster for the Atlanta Braves, he was asked to pick a number smaller than the 71 he had originally been assigned. He picked 22, to honor his high school catcher.

Andy Wilmot, Tammie Ruston's only son, played on the same 2005 high school state championship team with Heyward. A year after the championship, Wilmot was killed in a car accident.

> "This is for [Tammie Ruston] and her son," Heyward told MLB.com on the eve of his major-league debut in 2010. "He was one of my teammates and one of my

good friends. This is not something I'm saying, 'Hey, look at me, and this is why I'm doing it.' It means something to me, and I knew it would mean something to her and it always will."

But when Heyward was acquired by the St. Louis Cardinals in a four-player trade in 2014, his decision posed a dilemma: Manager Mike Matheny not only wore 22 when he was a catcher for the Cardinals, but also as its manager. His charity is named Catch-22. But Matheny knew the story of why Heyward chose the number. That's why on opening day, 2015, number 22 was assigned to a right-fielder, not the manager.

This decision was not the only number change for the team. Matheny's new number is 26, the hockey number worn by Sean Glanvill, who died seven years after a traumatic brain injury suffered in a hockey game at the age of 12. Glanvill was the son of close friends of Matheny. That meant closer Trevor Rosenthal, already wearing 26 on his uniform, switched to 44, which had been worn by Carlos Martinez. Had been?

During the off-season, Carlos Martinez was given permission to change his number from 44 to 18, the number worn by his teammate and close friend Oscar Taveras, who was killed in a car accident shortly after the end of the 2014 season.

If all of this makes you dizzy, it should. Changing the number you are assigned as a professional baseball player is not only unusual, but expensive. Baseball jerseys and t-shirts are a lucrative source of income, and players are expected to purchase the inventory of shirts with their old numbers. But that expense did not dissuade any of the Cardinals from honoring their friends.

As you've seen, one of the best ways to channel grief after the death of a friend is to find a way to honor them. In addition to changing the number you wear on your uniform, you might set up a scholarship fund, or challenge yourself to do something you know they wanted you to do.

And sometimes, you find yourself planning their memorial service.

Craig Winter and David Beckwith worked together at Art Institute of Colorado in Denver from 2000 to 2013. Winter was a pastry chef and ice carver extraordinaire, as evidenced by his 6 foot tall ice Stanley Cup celebrating Denver's championship. Beckwith was stronger in education, Winter stronger in baking and pastry. In Beckwith's mind, they made a strong, if odd team of culinary teachers:

> Big, burly, greying guy, straight as an arrow and of course me, the gay guy. He never, never had an issue with that. [His nickname for me] was "Tink". And never get between him and "Tink". You would pay! But it worked.

For years Winter was challenged by various forms of cancer. It would appear, he'd fight it, beat it back and return to teaching. The last time it hit hard. After losing seventy-five pounds, he finally had to quit teaching, remaining mostly bed-ridden. This didn't happen quickly: he'd been sick off and on for years, and his final illness ran over eight months. Beckwith visited often, unlike most others from their school.

Finally, hospice was called. Beckwith planned to visit his friend that Wednesday, but his teaching schedule interfered. So he showed up the next day, only to be greeted by Winter's wife who said, "Get up there now. It's time." And it was. Even though you know the time is close, even though your friend is in hospice care, you never really expect to witness their death.

Normally the family is responsible for holding a funeral or memorial service, but in this case, both Winter and his wife had asked Beckwith to take charge.

> Weird, that pressure to pull off a party for a man you loved as a friend and mentor and get it right. Get it right for the other folks, too.

Honored as he was, it wasn't easy:

> One could suppose I got lucky that I got to plan the sendoff. Not so…pressure to make it right for Julie and Craig. Pressure to comfort the others, pressure to comfort the students. Pressure to include the wanna-be friends, "as he was so important to me." Bull shit. You didn't visit, cause you didn't have the time? I spent an hour each way on trains and buses and you drive! You could have made it! I got more and more pissed off. I even had to call friends to check in that I was not losing it and had this in perspective.

Was it a success? Of course it was. He had calls from colleagues, students and former students offering to help in whatever way they could to honor Winter. Julie was pleased, and he believes Winter would've been too. But his anger lingers, reserved for those who managed to make his friend's death all about them. Some even admitted their offers were made because they felt guilty about not visiting him before he died.

When we don't feel we have the luxury of grieving, that grief can be channeled in a way that's fairly common: you don't have time to think about what you're feeling, because you're so busy "doing" for other people. And while it's sometimes necessary

– especially in a work setting – it's not always good on a personal level.

> Interesting, few of these if any ever asked how I was doing with losing Craig. I am not sure when or if I have mourned the losing of Craig. Maybe I did, and maybe I got what I needed for closure to start. By being there at the end and planning his celebration of life.

> I suspect this is all a delicate balance. But I do know, I was probably more fortunate than others with dealing with the death of a coworker. At least I think so.

Friends and coworkers of those who died in the September 11 attacks on the World Trade Center have created fundraising events of all kinds, from fun runs to black-tie dinners. Some have started nonprofit organizations or changed their own careers, leaving the corporate world for something more personally fulfilling. Your tour guide at the 9/11 Memorial and Museum might very well be a survivor like Brian Branco, telling stories of the three coworkers he lost that day. Other 9/11 survivors offer assistance to people suffering traumatic loss, building on their own experience to help others heal.

When it's a friend you work with, honoring your friend can certainly be an individual decision, but it can also wind up being a group project.

In 1994, the St. Louis law firm Armstrong Teasdale hired a summer associate named Michael C. Tramble, a young African-American veteran from the University of Missouri law school. Two years later, he was hired full-time.

> "He was a large man who always had this big smile on his face. He just lit up a room," said Rick Engel,

who was Tramble's mentor at the firm. After just a few minutes in a room with Tramble, it became clear, Engle said: "Yeah, I want to hang with that guy." Engle and Tramble became close friends, as did their wives.

But one day in the summer of 1998, the always-reliable Tramble failed to show up for work. The next day, police called the office, asking for someone to come to Tramble's home. Engel and the firm's managing partner drove there, prepared for the worst. They got it.

Tramble's wife's ex-husband, with whom she'd been involved in a bitter custody dispute, had murdered them and their two children and then killed himself.

"When something bad like that happens, you try to figure out what the absolute right thing to do is, and there is no answer to that," admitted Richard Sherrer, the managing partner, in a video posted on the firm's intranet.

Ultimately, the members of the firm decided to offer scholarships to minorities attending Tramble's alma mater. And although with each year, there are fewer people at Armstrong Teasdale who remember Michael Tramble, the firm has managed to turn their tribute into a company-wide fundraiser that includes a chili cook-off and a dessert auction. Everyone there has a chance to do something positive, something fun, that brings them together in memory of a promising young lawyer who left them much too soon.

Sometimes the coworker actually has an idea of how they want to be remembered. Bob Fosse, ever the control freak, left very specific instructions for his memorial service before his cardiac bypass years before his death:

> I give and bequest the sum of $25,000 to be distributed to the friends of mine listed…so that when my friends receive this bequest they will go out and have dinner on me.

There were sixty-six people on the list ($378.79 each). But his control didn't end there. They were required to donate the money back to a party fund, making them investors in an event no one would want to miss. He was going to control their last memory of him.

More than two hundred people showed up at Tavern on the Green: most of them coworkers at some time: Liza Minnelli, Roy Scheider, Neil Simon, Dianne Wiest, Elia Kazan, Stanley Donen. They were his legacy, proof of the talent he sometimes doubted, charged now with keeping his memory and importance alive.

It was a great party, which I'm sure he would've thoroughly enjoyed and then mercilessly critiqued. The band was still going strong at midnight, though most of the guests were gone. A few of those left paid their own tribute to Fosse, in the way they knew best, the way he taught them:

> Suddenly Ben Vereen flew to the dance floor. He threw his hands into the air and then onto his hips and started slithering. At first he was alone, but moments later the crowd caught on. [Ann] Reinking followed with [his daughter] Nicole and the eternal redhead, Nicole's mother, the Empress [Gwen Verdon]. The bandleader upped the tempo to a funk sound with the kind of heavy percussion Fosse loved, and Fosse's

three women moved closer together. Verdon, sixty-two; Reinking, thirty-eight; and Nicole, twenty-four – wife, mistress, daughter – started swaying, their arms entwined, moving together in an unmistakably sensual, sexy way. Their eyes closed and their bodies merged with the beat, pulsing together, like a hot human heart. Others joined them. First ex-girlfriends, then writers. A circle formed, closing in around the women, then opened, then closed, ceaselessly breaking apart and coming together. Grief and laughter poured out of them in waves.

The Sisters of Loretto tribute to the working relationship and friendship between their community and Thomas Merton was, not surprisingly, less ostentatious. Sister Mary Luke Tobin recalled:

I remember Merton's saying, during the last year of his life, "I'd like to see a center started where creative exchange could take place among contemplatives, activists, intellectuals, persons of various professions and disciplines, people whose ideas can help each other grow toward new insights. It could be located at Loretto, for example, and I'd be willing to help implement it." Of course, such a center was not begun at Loretto, and he did not live to facilitate it.

The Thomas Merton Center for Creative Exchange, a chapter of the International Thomas Merton Society, was her answer to how best continue the work of her friend. Founded in 1979, it fosters the types of spiritual and intellectual conversations on the topics closest to Merton.

And sometimes preserving a memory is as simple as what Monsignor Velo learned from his friendship with his boss, Cardinal Bernardin: living your life with transparence and dedication, being at ease with all kinds of people. He also learned the virtue of planning ahead: Bernardin was only sixty-eight when he died. The preparation eased the anxiety of those left behind: the Cardinal even did his Christmas shopping in July, leaving Velo's gift and a thank you note in his desk.

Although Cantor Fitzgerald survived, in the aftermath of 9/11 many businesses in the World Trade Center were lost, including the iconic Windows on the World restaurant, located on the 106th and 107th floors of the north tower. Michael Lomonaco was its executive chef and director. In one of the many strange stories of that day, he made it out because he was in the lobby having his glasses fixed when the towers were hit.

He, along with other employees who survived, created Windows of Hope, a fund to support the health and educational needs of their colleagues' families, including one child born that day.

When he opened a restaurant called Noche in 2002, he hired forty former employees, but it took five years after the attacks, when he opened Porter House New York, before he finally was able to recreate the family-like atmosphere of their former restaurant. As the tenth anniversary neared, Lomonaco explained how the attacks that killed seventy-three of his coworkers changed him:

> I try to focus on how much I love what I do and how my colleagues and friends who died, died loving what they did. Working at Windows was something they were proud of. I've spent every day since acknowledging and dedicating the work I do to friends I lost on that day.

So What Are We to Do?

Most people prefer to hear of a friend's death in private. It adds to the shock to learn about it from a news report on TV, hear it on the radio or in a voice mail, see it on your Facebook notifications or open up an email announcing a friend's death. Employers can struggle with how to share sudden news like this with their employees, clients and customers.

The protocols following the death of an employee should be part of every business' crisis management plan – assuming, of course, that they have a crisis management plan.

Most people don't consider this when writing a business plan. They're too busy in the start-up process to take time to plan for a crisis. Securing funding, creating a marketing campaign, finding a location, hiring employees – that's where their energies are focused. Once the business is up and running and has achieved some stability, their focus shifts to ensuring steady streams of income and planning for growth.

That's why companies large and small are so vulnerable when bad things happen. They call in a crisis management team afterwards – something that may have been unnecessary if they had just planned for the bad stuff that happens to us all.

I mentioned earlier about institutional memory: people who have been around a long time and just know stuff. Many businesses run for years – decades – without writing down policies or procedures. Maybe they had little staff turnover. Maybe they just passed down traditions in an oral history that eventually everyone "knew."

We've all seen them, the trappings of a firefighter's funeral: black and purple bunting draping the entrance to the station, bagpipers and drummers escorting the funeral procession. Those rituals – and the logistics – were not written down until the summer of 2001, just months before the terrorist attacks on the World Trade Center.

With such a loss of life – 343 men – the need for those rituals was overwhelming. For example, when a New York City firefighter died in the line of duty, the station that suffered the most recent loss was responsible for providing the meal after the funeral. With the staggering losses of September 11, that was almost impossible. Other logistics – where to get the bunting, what songs should the pipers play – now written down, made the over four hundred funerals and memorial services easier to plan. Why so many? Memorial services were often held before remains were recovered; funerals afterwards. Some families opted for both.

The possibility of a line of duty death is one that's accepted by everyone who enlists in the military or becomes a first responder. Establishing rituals, and making sure that the details are known by everyone, can go a long way towards helping coworkers deal with their grief. There is, even for those who are not in a dangerous line of work, a shared comfort in rituals.

Most people don't want to think about death, whether it's their own or that of someone close to them. Many businesses lack a succession plan, because the boss assumes they'll be around forever.

So it is with dealing with a death in the workplace. You just don't want to think about it. Honestly, who does? But as we've seen time and again – with our families and others – even a little bit of planning eases the grief of those left behind.

This is by no means a comprehensive list. And I hope that you never have reason to make use of it. But here are some suggestions for honoring the memory of a coworker:

- Leave flowers on their desk.

- Create a "shrine": a photo collage or a plaque near the entrance to your workplace or the area where they worked.

- Hold an employee luncheon where there are no formal speeches, just informal reflections.

- Recognize that person company-wide: in an employee newsletter, video-conference call, email blast.

- Establish a scholarship fund in their name.

- Make a donation to an organization they loved.

- Invite customers to share their memories.

- Set up a formal memorial service.

- Create a Facebook memorial page, so that coworkers can share their grief.

- Keep in close contact with surviving family members.

How a tragedy like this is handled reflects not only on the management team but the culture of the organization. How an employee death is dealt with – the immediate response, the support for the remaining employees and recognition of that person – will be remembered for years to come.

In one workplace, an employee died without life insurance or a will, leaving their family in considerable financial distress. The boss made it his mission to ensure that every one of his employees had both, going as far as subsidizing the cost of writing a will. You can bet that that's a company whose employees look favorably on management.

After Randy Salerno's death, WBBM was inundated with thousands of cards and emails from viewers. One of the employees bound them all together for the family. Tellez herself received several hundred emails. It took months, but she answered each one personally, because she knew how much her partnership with Salerno had meant to their audience.

Every workplace is different, just as every friendship is different. So before you dismiss the suggestions above as impractical or unlikely, take the time to reflect on how your friend would want to be remembered. Let them – and your friendship – be your guide.

Lynne McCollum Staley's grief shook her to her bones. It wasn't just grief for the loss of a dear friend, a young wife and mother. It went far deeper. She wrote and published *In Death is the Secret to Life: A Tribute Journal* to help people both grieve and celebrate life. A beautifully constructed book, the journal includes quotes to help friends and family members share joyful memories as well as sadness.

> I became a student of the subject of grief and loss. I published the *Tribute Journal* and knew that there was

more to my healing grief journey. I continued to be struck by how people didn't know how to show up for those who were grieving. Though initially put off by the word "recovery" in the book's title, I read *The Grief Recovery Handbook* and was compelled to become certified to facilitate The Grief Recovery Method ™.

She left her work in development and communications to work with people who are grieving. While it wasn't something Trici Brennan-Zuba asked her to do, she feels her friend guided her to this new, unexpected calling.

Roseanne Tellez decided to use the example of the man she referred to as "the sun in the solar system" as a guide for her own life, both personally and professionally. She took to heart his insistence "don't sweat making a mistake." She copied his style of asking lots of questions. She helped create an event in his memory to raise money for muscular dystrophy.

When I interviewed her, nearly two years after Salerno's death, she insisted she hadn't felt his presence since he died. Given the depth of their friendship, I found that surprising. But not long after, I received an email from her. Apparently, there was one time.

Tellez had just returned to work after her mother's funeral. When she sat down at her computer, it appeared that some windows were open. When she shut one down, a full-screen picture of Salerno appeared, staring at her with a huge grin. She was so startled she pushed her chair back from the desk.

It was weird for this picture to be up. I had not even opened my email page yet and there was this nearly two-year-old open email that a coworker had sent after Randy's death. At this moment I felt like Randy was in the room saying, "Lighten up, Tellez. It'll be alright."

Life goes on without our friends. Sometimes work goes on, too. And though it will take a long time, it'll be alright.

Acknowledgements

To those who were so generous with their time, especially David Beckwith, Lynne McCollum Staley, Roseanne Tellez and Monsignor Kenneth Velo.

To my statistician, Lynn McSorley, a special shout-out.

To the friends I worked with who are no longer here: bosses, coworkers, volunteers.

To my family, for their patience.

References

Buffa, Dan. "12 Years Later: Darryl Kile's Legacy Still Going Strong," *KSDK.com,* June 23, 2014.

The Effect of Work Relationships on Organizational Culture and Commitment, Globoforce Fall 2014 Report, Workforce Mood Tracker Survey, September, 2014.

Flippen, Alan, "No, Celebrity Deaths Do Not Comes in Threes." *New York Times,* August 14, 2014.

Gilvey, John Anthony. *Before the Parade Passes By: Gower Champion and the Glorious American Musical,* St. Martin's Press, New York, 2005.

Goodman, Michelle. "Death in the Workplace: How to Cope," *abcnews.com,* Nov. 19, 2009.

Goold, Derrick. "Why Heyward will wear No. 22 for Cardinals," *St. Louis Post-Dispatch,* November 24, 2014.

Sideman, Amanda P., "Chef's uptown eatery a personal 9/11 memorial for friends lost at Windows on the World." *NY Daily News,* July 24, 2011.

Leibovich, Mark. *This Town: Two Parties and a Funeral – plus plenty of valet parking! – in America's Gilded Capital.* Blue Rider Press, a member of Penguin Group USA, New York, 2014.

Moore, Doug. "Law Firm Honors Memory of Beloved Associate," *St. Louis Post-Dispatch*, February 1, 2015.

Strauss, Joe. "Kile's Death Still Shakes Those Who Were Close to Him," *St. Louis Post-Dispatch*, June 18, 2012.

Thurston, Bonnie, General Editor. *Hidden in the Same Mystery: Thomas Merton and Loretto.* Fons Vitae, Louisville, KY, 2010.

Wasson, Sam. *Fosse.* Houghton Mifflin Harcourt Publishing, New York, 2013.

Wilkes, Paul, ed. *Merton: By Those Who Knew Him Best.* Harper & Row Publishers, San Francisco, 1984

Young, Neil. *Waging Heavy Peace*, Penguin Group USA. New York, 2013.

Resources

Companies interested in addressing the unique needs following the death of an employee will find everything they need in the following books, available from their publishers and online.

Grief in the Workplace: A Comprehensive Guide to Being Prepared, by Rachel Blythe Kodanaz. GIW Publishing, Denver, Co, 2015.

Healing Grief at Work: 100 Practical Ideas After Your Workplace is Touched by Loss, by Alan D. Wolfelt, PhD. Companion Press, Fort Collins, CO, 2005.

Books by Victoria Noe

Friend Grief and Anger: When Your Friend Dies and No One Gives A Damn

Friend Grief and AIDS: Thirty Years of Burying Our Friends

Friend Grief and 9/11: The Forgotten Mourners

Friend Grief and the Military: Band of Friends

Victoria Noe has been a writer most of her life, but didn't admit it until 2009. After earning a masters degree in Speech and Dramatic Art from the University of Iowa, she moved to Chicago, where she worked professionally as a stage manager, director and administrator in addition to being a founding board member of the League of Chicago Theatres. She then transferred her skills to being a professional fundraiser, raising money for arts, educational and AIDS service organizations, and later an award-winning sales consultant of children's books. Noe also trained hundreds of people around the country in marketing, event planning and grant writing. But after a concussion impacted her ability to continue in sales, she switched gears to keep a promise to a dying friend to write a book.

That book is now an award-winning series. The first three – *Friend Grief and Anger: When Your Friend Dies and No One Gives A Damn*; *Friend Grief and AIDS: Thirty Years of Burying Our Friends* and *Friend Grief and 9/11: The Forgotten Mourners* were published in 2013. Following *Friend Grief and the Military:*

Band of Friends was published in 2014. The final books in the series will be published in 2015 – *Friend Grief in the Workplace: More Than an Empty Cubicle* and *Friend Grief and Men: Defying Stereotypes.*

Noe is a member of Alliance of Independent Authors (ALLI), Chicago Writers Association, Nonfiction Authors Association, Military Writers Society of America and ACT UP/NY. Her freelance articles have appeared on numerous grief and writing blogs as well as *Windy City Times, Chicago Tribune* and *Huffington Post.* In addition, she feeds her reading habit by reviewing a wide variety of books on BroadwayWorld.com. A native St. Louisan, she's a lifelong Cardinals fan and will gladly take on any comers in musical theatre trivia. Her blog, www.FriendGrief.com, was named one of the top ten grief support websites in 2012.

For more information on what she's up to, including public speaking, go to www.victorianoe.com.